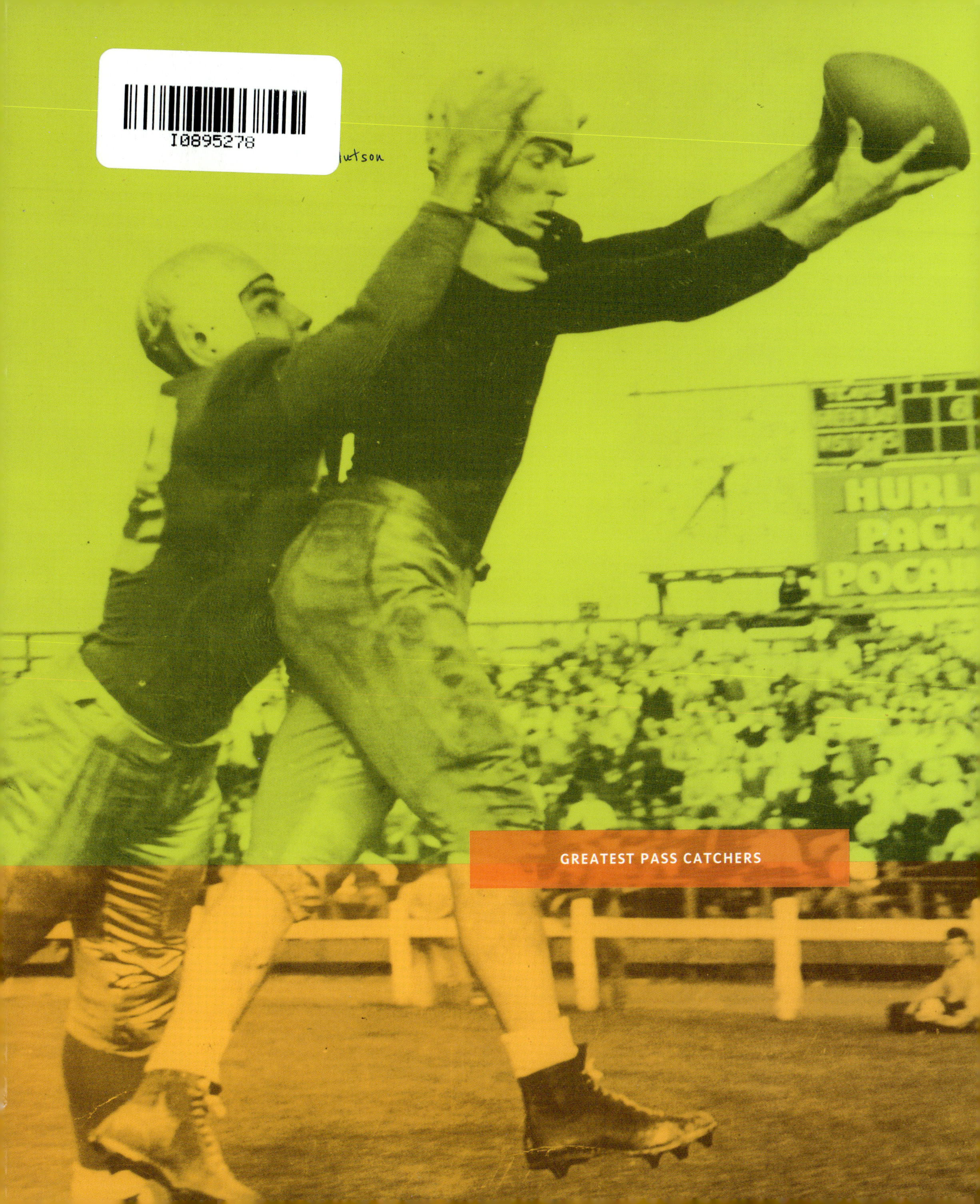

GREATEST PASS CATCHERS

Randy Moss

NFL HALL OF FAMERS

GREATEST PASS CATCHERS

JOE TISCHLER

Marvin Harrison

CREATIVE SPORTS

CREATIVE EDUCATION / CREATIVE PAPERBACKS

Published by Creative Education and Creative Paperbacks
P.O. Box 227, Mankato, Minnesota 56002
Creative Education and Creative Paperbacks
are imprints of The Creative Company
www.thecreativecompany.us

Design and production by Blue Design (www.bluedes.com)
Art direction by Rita Marshall

Images by Associated Press/Betty Kumpf, 14; Getty Images/Allen Kee, 21, Andy Hayt, 9, Andy Lyons, 18, Bill Eppridge/Time Life Pictures, 7, Bob Leverone/Sporting News Archive, 25, Brad Mangin, 17, Charles Aqua Viva, 12, Chris Graythen, 3, 22, DAVE KAUP, 29, Diamond Images, 4–5, 32, Focus On Sport, 6, 7, Gregory Shamus, 7, 30, Jamie Squire, 26, 28, Kidwiler Collection, 7, Michael Zagaris, 6, NFL/Pro Football Hall of Fame, 6, Pro Football Hall of Fame, 1, Rob Tringali, 2, TIMOTHY A. CLARY, 6, Tom Hauck, cover, Tom Pidgeon, 19; NFL/Corky Charles Trewin/WireImage.com, 15; Wikimedia Commons/Gonzo fan2007, cover (background), public domain, 10, 11

Library of Congress Cataloging-in-Publication Data
Names: Tischler, Joe, author.
Title: Greatest pass catchers / Joe Tischler.
Description: Mankato, Minnesota : Creative Education and Creative Paperbacks, [2026] | Series: Creative sports: NFL hall of famers | Includes index. | Audience: Ages 8–12 | Audience: Grades 4–6 | Summary: "Photo-driven and stat-filled, this middle-grade NFL title showcases 11 of pro football's greatest pass catchers enshrined in the Hall of Fame, from Don Hutson and Jerry Rice to Randy Moss and Calvin Johnson"—Provided by publisher.
Identifiers: LCCN 2024048111 (print) | LCCN 2024048112 (ebook) | ISBN 9798889896159 (library binding) | ISBN 9781682777817 (paperback) | ISBN 9798889896951 (ebook)
Subjects: LCSH: Football players—United States—Biography—Juvenile literature. | Football—United States—Juvenile literature. | National Football League—Juvenile literature.
Classification: LCC GV939.A1 T57 2026 (print) | LCC GV939.A1 (ebook) | DDC 796.332092/2 [B]—dc23/eng/20231122
LC record available at https://lccn.loc.gov/2024048111
LC ebook record available at https://lccn.loc.gov/2024048112

Printed in India

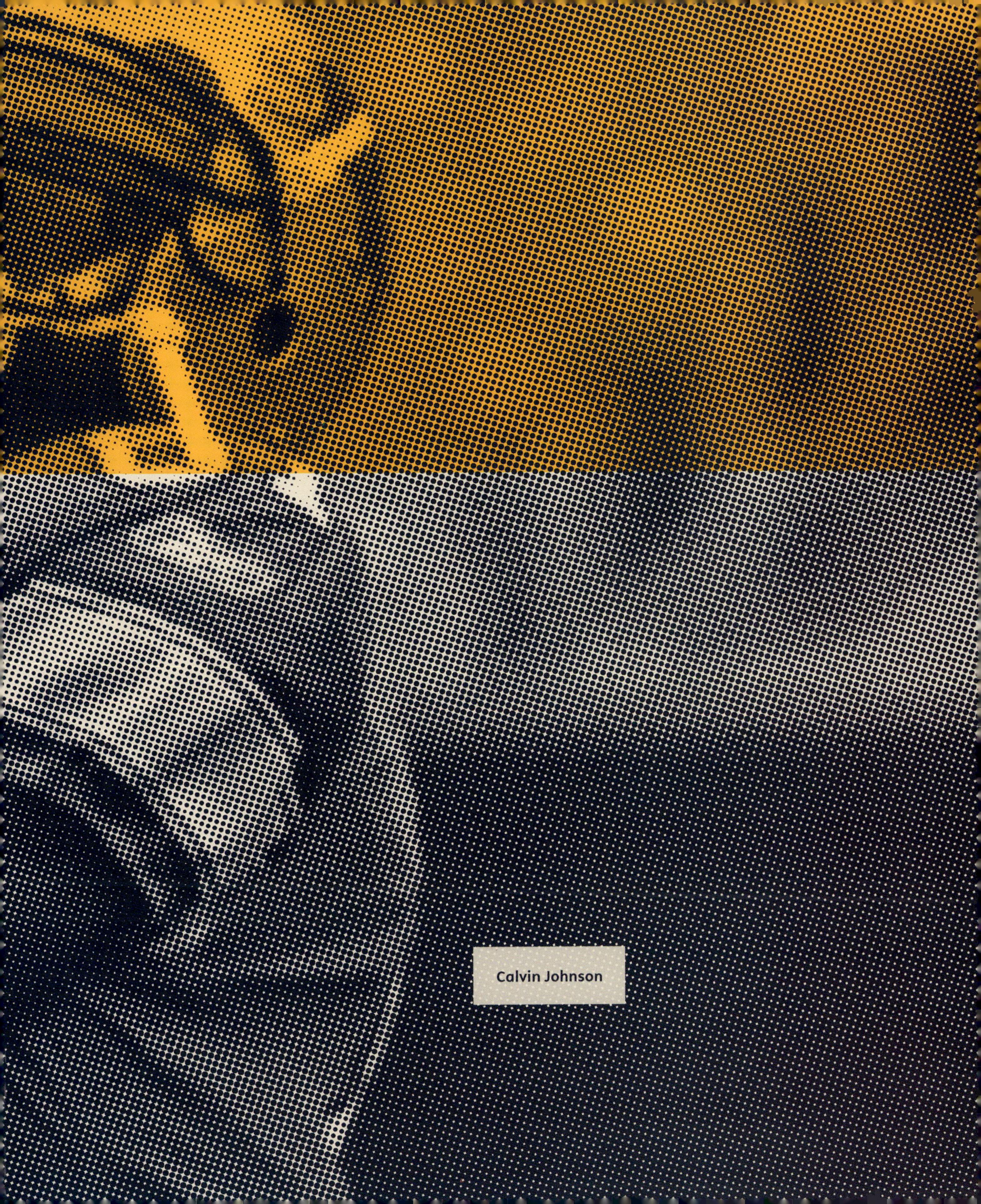

Calvin Johnson

60

MOSS
81

TAYLOR
56

42

CONTENTS

TIMEOUT

INTRODUCTION

The San Francisco 49ers have the ball on the Los Angeles Raiders' 38-yard line. Quarterback Steve Young drops back to pass. He lofts the ball deep down the center of the field. Wide receiver Jerry Rice is double covered, but it doesn't matter. Rice easily leaps and snatches the ball. Touchdown!

Tight ends and wide receivers make up football's pass catchers. They have fast legs, sure hands, and a sharp sense of space and direction. All pass catchers who play for the National Football League (NFL) are at the top of their game. But only a handful can be called Hall of Famers.

The Pro Football Hall of Fame honors 378 past players, coaches, and sport contributors. Of those, just over 50 are wide receivers/tight ends. This book highlights 11 Hall of Fame pass catchers whose careers reached above and beyond. This list isn't a ranking. Players are ordered by the year they were enshrined.

Jerry Rice

DON HUTSON (1913–97)
END, SAFETY, KICKER
GREEN BAY PACKERS SEASONS: 1935–45
HALL OF FAME CLASS: 1963
AWARDS/HONORS: MEMBER OF NFL 50TH/75TH/100TH ANNIVERSARY TEAMS, 8X FIRST TEAM ALL-PRO, 4X PRO BOWL, 1930S NFL ALL-DECADE TEAM, 2X NFL MOST VALUABLE PLAYER, 3X NFL CHAMPION

DON HUTSON

Don Hutson is considered one of football's first great pass catchers. When he retired from the Green Bay Packers in 1945, he held 18 NFL records. They included career receptions, receiving yards, and receiving touchdowns. Many of those records held for decades. Hutson finished with 99 career touchdown receptions. That NFL record stood until 1989.

Hutson led the league in receptions eight times in his 11-year career. Seven times he led the league in receiving yards. Nine times he led the league in touchdown receptions. Hutson was also a good defensive player. He started playing defensive back in 1940. That year, he led the league with six interceptions. He snatched 30 interceptions in six seasons playing defense. Hutson was a kicker, too. When he scored a touchdown, he would kick his own extra points. Hutson led the league in scoring five times.

Twice in his career, Hutson was awarded the Joe F. Carr Trophy. It was given to the NFL's Most Valuable Player. Hutson was a key member of three Packers NFL championship teams (1936, 1939, 1944). He was inducted as a charter member of the Pro Football Hall of Fame in 1963. He was also a member of the NFL 50th, 75th, and 100th anniversary teams.

Don Hutson

PASS CATCHER DUTIES

Wide receivers are usually the fastest players on offense. They are the main targets for quarterbacks on passing plays. They run passing routes at varying lengths. They try to create separation from their defenders before the pass comes their way. Generally, there are two to four wide receivers on each play. They line up closer to the sidelines on either side of the quarterback. Tight ends generally line up at the end of the offensive line on either side. They weigh more than wide receivers. They can stay in and block or run passing routes like the wide receivers.

19
24

LANCE ALWORTH

LANCE ALWORTH (1940–)
WIDE RECEIVER
SAN DIEGO CHARGERS SEASONS: 1962–70; DALLAS COWBOYS SEASONS: 1971–72
HALL OF FAME CLASS: 1978
AWARDS/HONORS: MEMBER OF NFL 75TH/100TH ANNIVERSARY TEAMS, 7X ALL-PRO (6X FIRST TEAM), 7X PRO BOWL, AFL PLAYER OF THE YEAR, AFL CHAMPION, SUPER BOWL CHAMPION

Late in his career, Lance Alworth won a Super Bowl championship with the Dallas Cowboys. Before then, he was one of the best wide receivers in American Football League (AFL) history. His nickname was "Bambi." He could run as quickly and gracefully as a deer. Alworth did not play much in his first season with San Diego (1962). He caught only 10 passes. He caught a lot more in 1963. He had 61 receptions for 1,205 yards and 11 touchdowns. The United Press International named him AFL Player of the Year. The Chargers won 11 games and won the AFL championship. That season marked the first of Alworth's seven straight AFL All-Star Game appearances.

Alworth led the AFL in touchdown receptions in 1964. He grabbed 13 in just 12 games. He led the league again the following two seasons. In 1965, he had 14 touchdown receptions. He also led the league in receiving yards with 1,602. Alworth earned the AFL receiving triple crown in 1966, leading the league in receptions (73), receiving yards (1,383), and touchdown receptions (13). He would lead the league in receptions and receiving yards again in 1968.

The AFL merged with the NFL in 1970. Alworth played his final two seasons with Dallas. He caught a touchdown pass in Super Bowl VI (6) as the Cowboys beat the Miami Dolphins, 24–3. Alworth became the first AFL player to be elected to the Pro Football Hall of Fame.

STEVE LARGENT

STEVE LARGENT (1954–)
WIDE RECEIVER
SEATTLE SEAHAWKS SEASONS: 1976–89
HALL OF FAME CLASS: 1995
AWARDS/HONORS: MEMBER OF NFL 100TH ANNIVERSARY TEAM, 5X ALL-PRO (1X FIRST TEAM), 7X PRO BOWL, 1980S NFL ALL-DECADE TEAM, NFL MAN OF THE YEAR

Steve Largent's Hall of Fame career nearly ended before it began. The Houston Oilers selected Largent in the fourth round of the 1976 NFL Draft. At the end of the preseason, the Oilers were going to cut Largent. Instead, they traded him to the expansion Seattle Seahawks. Largent was grateful for the new opportunity. He went on to a stellar 14-year Hall of Fame career. At the time he retired, he held six NFL receiving records. They included most career receptions (819), most career receiving yards (13,089), and most career touchdown receptions (100).

Largent had his first 1,000-yard receiving season in 1978. The following year, he led the league in receiving yards with 1,237. He would lead the league in the same category again in 1985. In between, he was a man of consistency. He retired with the NFL record for most consecutive games with a reception with 177. Largent is the first player in NFL history to catch 100 touchdown passes in a career. He was selected for seven Pro Bowls. He was also an All-Pro selection five times.

Largent made his mark off the field, too. He won the NFL Man of the Year award in 1988. The award is given for community involvement. After his playing career, Largent went into politics. He served in the U.S. House of Representatives. He represented Oklahoma's first congressional district from 1994 to 2002.

JERRY RICE

JERRY RICE (1962–)
WIDE RECEIVER
SAN FRANCISCO 49ERS SEASONS: 1985–2000; OAKLAND RAIDERS SEASONS: 2001–04; SEATTLE SEAHAWKS SEASON: 2004
HALL OF FAME CLASS: 2010
AWARDS/HONORS: MEMBER OF NFL 75TH/100TH ANNIVERSARY TEAMS, 11X ALL-PRO (10X FIRST TEAM), 13X PRO BOWL, 1980S/1990S NFL ALL-DECADE TEAMS, 2X NFL OFFENSIVE PLAYER OF THE YEAR, 3X SUPER BOWL CHAMPION, SUPER BOWL MVP

The San Francisco 49ers traded up in the 1985 NFL Draft. They did so to select a little-known wide receiver named Jerry Rice. It turned out to be one of the greatest draft trades in NFL history. To this day, Rice holds every major receiving record. He's the career leader in receptions (1,549). He's the career leader in receiving yards (22,895). And he's the career leader in receiving touchdowns (197). Rice also has the most career touchdowns with 208.

Rice started putting up big numbers in 1986. In just his second season, he led the league in receiving yards (1,570) and receiving touchdowns (15). Four times he led the league in those categories. One of his greatest seasons was 1987. Playing in only 12 games, due to a players' strike, Rice set an NFL record with 22 touchdown receptions. That record stood for 20 years. Rice was named NFL Offensive Player of the Year for the first time. While his regular seasons were great, Rice may have played his best in the Super Bowl. Following the 1988 season, he was named MVP of Super Bowl XXIII (23). He caught 11 passes for 215 yards and a touchdown. Over four Super Bowl games, he caught a record eight touchdown passes. That's three more than anybody else in Super Bowl history.

Rice led the league in receiving yards six times, including 1,848 yards in 1995. That was a single-season record that stood for 17 years. Rice played 20 years. No other wide receiver has played in the league longer than him.

Shannon Sharpe

POSITION CHANGES

The passing game has changed a lot in recent years. Quarterbacks often pass for more than 4,000 yards a season. As a result, teams need dynamic wide receivers and tight ends. The men in these positions have become football's primary playmakers. In today's game, they include Minnesota Vikings wide receiver Justin Jefferson, Miami Dolphins wide receiver Tyreek Hill, and Kansas City Chiefs tight end Travis Kelce. They are generally the first target of the quarterback on passing plays. Defenders, in turn, form game plans to contain them. That might mean putting two or even three defenders on a pass catcher to keep him from catching the ball.

SHANNON SHARPE (1968–)
TIGHT END
DENVER BRONCOS SEASONS: 1990–99, 2002–03; BALTIMORE RAVENS SEASONS: 2000–01
HALL OF FAME CLASS: 2011
AWARDS/HONORS: 5X ALL-PRO (4X FIRST TEAM), 8X PRO BOWL, 1990S NFL ALL-DECADE TEAM, 3X SUPER BOWL CHAMPION

SHANNON SHARPE

Only nine tight ends have been elected to the Pro Football Hall of Fame. Shannon Sharpe is one of them. Sharpe is one of the greatest pass catchers in NFL history. However, he may not be the best pass catcher in his family! Sharpe is the younger brother of Sterling Sharpe. Sterling played wide receiver for the Green Bay Packers from 1988 to 1994. He led the league in receptions three times. Unfortunately, his career was cut short due to a neck injury.

Shannon Sharpe did more than pick up the slack for his family. He was one of the favorite targets for Denver Broncos quarterback John Elway. Sharpe was a key member of Denver's Super Bowl championship teams in 1997 and 1998. He earned the first of his eight Pro Bowl nods in 1992. He earned three straight First Team All-Pro selections from 1996 to 1998. Sharpe had a career high in touchdown receptions with 10 in both 1996 and 1998.

Sharpe signed with the Baltimore Ravens in 2000. He helped his new team to their first Super Bowl title in his first season. He caught a 96-yard touchdown pass in the AFC Championship Game to help Baltimore reach the Super Bowl. That play is the longest playoff touchdown reception in NFL history. Sharpe returned to play for the Broncos his final two seasons before retiring in 2003. He led Denver in receptions six times in his career.

CRIS CARTER

CRIS CARTER (1965–)
WIDE RECEIVER
PHILADELPHIA EAGLES SEASONS: 1987–89; MINNESOTA VIKINGS SEASONS: 1990–2001; MIAMI DOLPHINS SEASON: 2002
HALL OF FAME CLASS: 2013
AWARDS/HONORS: 3X ALL-PRO (2X FIRST TEAM), 8X PRO BOWL, 1990S NFL ALL-DECADE TEAM, NFL MAN OF THE YEAR

Cris Carter's first career NFL reception was for a touchdown. He would catch a lot more throughout the next 16 years. He caught 110 of his 130 career touchdowns as a Minnesota Viking. He led the league in touchdown receptions three times, including a career-high 17 in 1995. Carter's 130 career touchdowns rank fourth all-time.

Carter got off to a slow start in 1987. The Philadelphia Eagles released him after three seasons due to off-field issues. But Carter turned his life around with Minnesota. He became very involved in community work. In 1993, he started putting up eye-catching numbers. He had his first 1,000-yard receiving season. The following year was historic. He set a then-NFL single-season record with 122 receptions. He hit that total in 1995 as well. Carter is one of only four players to record 120 receptions in a season twice. In 1999, he was named Walter Payton NFL Man of the Year. "I come from some humble beginnings," said Carter. "I just believed that when people pay their money, hard-earned money, that they deserve a certain level of performance."

Carter recorded eight straight 1,000-yard seasons with Minnesota. He also led the team in receptions for 10 straight seasons. The Vikings regularly made the playoffs with Carter as their main receiver. But they failed to reach the Super Bowl. Carter retired in 2002 as the NFL's second all-time leading receiver with 1,101 receptions.

Riddell
80

MARVIN HARRISON

MARVIN HARRISON (1972–)
WIDE RECEIVER
INDIANAPOLIS COLTS SEASONS: 1996–2008
HALL OF FAME CLASS: 2016
AWARDS/HONORS: MEMBER OF NFL 100TH ANNIVERSARY TEAM, 8X ALL-PRO (3X FIRST TEAM), 8X PRO BOWL, 2000S NFL ALL-DECADE TEAM, SUPER BOWL CHAMPION

Marvin Harrison and Peyton Manning formed one of the greatest wide receiver/quarterback combos in NFL history. The Indianapolis Colts duo played together for 11 years. In Manning's first year (1998), Harrison caught seven touchdown passes from him. The following year, the pair really took off. Harrison caught 115 passes for a league-leading 1,663 yards and 12 touchdowns. The Colts went from 3 wins in 1998 to 13 in 1999. Harrison continued to put up stellar numbers. He led the league in receptions in 2000 with 102. His 2002 season was off the charts. He shattered the NFL single-season receptions record with 143. The old record was 123. Harrison's new record stood for 17 seasons. Also in 2002, Harrison led the league in receiving yards for the second time with 1,722.

Harrison continued to record 1,000-yard receiving seasons through 2006. He caught 95 passes for 1,366 yards and 12 touchdowns. It was his eighth straight 1,000-yard receiving season. The Colts reached Super Bowl XLI (41) following the 2006 season. They defeated the Chicago Bears for the title.

Harrison finished his career with 1,102 receptions. That mark was second all-time when he retired after the 2008 season. He was also second all-time in consecutive games with a reception (190) and most career 100-yard receiving games (59). The Harrison-Manning combo connected for 953 career passes, 12,766 yards, and 112 touchdowns. All are most for a wide receiver-quarterback pair in NFL history.

RANDY MOSS

RANDY MOSS (1977–)
WIDE RECEIVER
MINNESOTA VIKINGS SEASONS: 1998–2004, 2010; OAKLAND RAIDERS SEASONS: 2005–06; NEW ENGLAND PATRIOTS SEASONS: 2007–10; TENNESSEE TITANS SEASON: 2010; SAN FRANCISCO 49ERS SEASON: 2012
HALL OF FAME CLASS: 2018
AWARDS/HONORS: MEMBER OF NFL 100TH ANNIVERSARY TEAM, 4X FIRST TEAM ALL-PRO, 6X PRO BOWL, 2000S NFL ALL-DECADE TEAM, NFL OFFENSIVE ROOKIE OF THE YEAR, NFL COMEBACK PLAYER OF THE YEAR

Randy Moss was one of the most athletic and talented wide receivers in pro football. He regularly went up high for passes and outran defenders. He was taken by the Minnesota Vikings with the 21st pick in the 1998 NFL Draft. And he took the league by storm. His mission was to make sure all the teams that had passed on him knew they had made the wrong choice. In his first career game, Moss caught two touchdown passes. He went on to snatch 17 touchdown passes that season, breaking an NFL rookie record. Moss caught 69 passes for 1,313 yards. He was named NFL Offensive Rookie of the Year. With Moss, the Vikings won 15 games in 1998. But they fell just shy of reaching the Super Bowl.

Moss kept putting up monster numbers in Minnesota. He recorded more than 1,000 receiving yards each of his first six seasons. The high mark came in 2003. He caught 111 passes for 1,632 yards and grabbed a league-high 17 touchdowns. Moss spent two subpar years with the Oakland Raiders before reviving his career with the New England Patriots in 2007. He set a single-season NFL record with 23 touchdown receptions. The Patriots were a perfect 16–0 in the regular season. But they fell to the New York Giants in Super Bowl XLII (42).

As of 2024, Moss ranks fourth all-time in receiving yards with 15,292. He's second all-time in touchdown receptions with 156.

TERRELL OWENS

TERRELL OWENS (1973–)
WIDE RECEIVER
SAN FRANCISCO 49ERS SEASONS: 1996–2003; PHILADELPHIA EAGLES SEASONS: 2004–05; DALLAS COWBOYS SEASONS: 2006–08; BUFFALO BILLS SEASON: 2009; CINCINNATI BENGALS SEASON: 2010
HALL OF FAME CLASS: 2018
AWARDS/HONORS: 5X FIRST TEAM ALL-PRO, 6X PRO BOWL, 2000S NFL ALL-DECADE TEAM

Terrell Owens joined the NFL in 1996. He played with the San Francisco 49ers. His first big moment came in the 1998 NFL Playoffs. It was a wild card game against the Green Bay Packers. Owens caught the game-winning 25-yard touchdown pass in the closing seconds. That year was his first 1,000-yard receiving season. He also caught 14 touchdown passes—two more than his first two seasons combined. In 2000, Owens had a career-high of 1,451 receiving yards. He also set a then-NFL single-game record with 20 receptions.

Owens signed with the Philadelphia Eagles in 2004. He had 1,200 receiving yards and 14 touchdowns. Late in the regular season, he broke his leg. The Eagles advanced to Super Bowl XXXIX (39). Owens came back to play in the game with a screw in his leg. He caught nine passes for 122 yards. But the Eagles came up short of winning the title. Owens played for the Dallas Cowboys from 2006 to 2008. Each year, he recorded at least 1,000 receiving yards. He snatched a league-high 13 touchdown passes in 2006.

Owens had at least 60 catches in 12 of his 15 NFL seasons. He had more than 1,000 receiving yards nine times and at least 10 touchdown receptions eight times. Owens ranks third all-time in touchdown receptions with 153. He also ranks third all-time with receiving yards with 15,934. Owens is eighth all-time in receptions with 1,078.

TONY GONZALEZ

TONY GONZALEZ (1976–)
TIGHT END
KANSAS CITY CHIEFS SEASONS: 1997–2008; ATLANTA FALCONS SEASONS: 2009–13
HALL OF FAME CLASS: 2019
AWARDS/HONORS: MEMBER OF NFL 100TH ANNIVERSARY TEAM, 10X ALL-PRO (6X FIRST TEAM), 14X PRO BOWL, 2000S NFL ALL-DECADE TEAM

Tony Gonzalez played football and basketball at the University of California. He had to make a choice which sport to pursue as a professional. He picked football. It was a good choice. Gonzalez turned out to be one of the greatest tight ends of all time.

The Kansas City Chiefs selected Gonzalez in the first round of the 1997 NFL Draft. He caught only four touchdown passes over his first two seasons. But the numbers started to go up in his third season. He caught 76 passes for 849 yards and 11 touchdowns in 1999. He made the first of his 14 Pro Bowls. And he was named to his first of 10 All-Pro teams. Gonzalez recorded his first 1,000-yard season in 2000. He collected 1,203 yards on 93 catches. His best season may have been 2004. He led the league with 102 receptions. That was an NFL single-season record for a tight end. He hit a career-high with 1,258 receiving yards and caught 7 touchdowns.

The Atlanta Falcons traded for Gonzalez in 2009. He continued to make Pro Bowl and All-Pro teams with his new squad. He caught 93 passes for Atlanta in 2012 as the Falcons reached the NFC Championship Game. Gonzalez retired after the 2013 season. He ranks third all-time with 1,325 career receptions. That is the most for a tight end. He ranks sixth all-time in receiving yards with 15,127. No other tight end has that many.

300 YARDS

The 300-yard receiving game is a very rare feat. In more than 100 years of professional football, it has been done only six times. The record was set by Willie “Flipper” Anderson of the Los Angeles Rams in 1989. He caught 15 passes for 336 yards and 1 touchdown in an overtime win over the New Orleans Saints. Hall of Famer Calvin Johnson is second on the list. He was just short of breaking the record in 2013. In a Detroit Lions win over the Dallas Cowboys, Johnson caught 14 passes for 329 yards and a touchdown.

CALVIN JOHNSON

CALVIN JOHNSON (1985–)
WIDE RECEIVER
DETROIT LIONS SEASONS: 2007–15
HALL OF FAME CLASS: 2021
AWARDS/HONORS: 4X ALL-PRO (3X FIRST TEAM), 6X PRO BOWL, 2010S NFL ALL-DECADE TEAM

In the Transformers toy world, Megatron is a fearsome giant robot. "Megatron" was also wide receiver Calvin Johnson's nickname. He had big hands, a big frame, and he played with a robot-like ability. He was taken as the second overall pick of the 2007 NFL Draft by the Detroit Lions. In 2008, his second season, Johnson caught 78 passes for 1,331 yards. He also landed a league-leading 12 touchdown receptions. The Lions, though, did not win a game that season. They were the first team ever to remain winless for a full 16-game season.

Detroit would eventually get better. Johnson had a lot to do with that. He led the league in receiving yards in 2011 with 1,681. He also caught a career-high 16 touchdown passes. With his help, the Lions won 10 games and made the playoffs. The following year was a historic season for Johnson. He led the league with 122 receptions. Those receptions added up to an NFL single-season record of 1,964 receiving yards. Johnson set another NFL record that season with eight straight 100-yard receiving games. He added 1,492 yards in 2013. His 5,137 receiving yards from 2011 to 2013 are the most by any wide receiver in history over a three-year span.

Johnson continued to impress following that three-year span. He had more than 1,000 yards receiving in both 2014 and 2015. He caught 88 passes for 1,214 yards in 2015. The following season, he unexpectedly retired. His 88 receptions are second most for a player in his final season.

INDEX